THE LIFESKILLS LIBRARY

Hearing the Pitch

Evaluating All Kinds of Advertising

Carlienne Frisch

THE ROSEN PUBLISHING GROUP, INC.

NEW YORK

Published in 1994 by The Rosen Publishing Group, Inc.
29 East 21st Street, New York, NY 10010

First Edition

Manufactured in the United States of America

Library of Congress Cataloging-in-Publication Data

Frisch, Carlienne.
    Hearing the Pitch: Evaluating all kinds of advertising / Carlienne Frisch—1st ed.
        p. cm. — (Lifeskills)
    Includes bibliographical references and index.
    ISBN 0-8239-1694-4
    1. Advertising—Juvenile literature. [1. Advertising.] I. Title II. Series: Life skills library.
    HF5821.F73   1994
    659.1—dc20   93-46200
                                                              CIP
                                                              AC

CONTENTS

INTRODUCTION

We see and hear advertising many times each day. Our favorite magazine has a photo of a popular rock star wearing expensive designer jeans. When we ride the city bus we see signs in the bus and on the buildings we are passing. The signs tell us many different things. One sign states that riding the bus is good for the environment. The next sign tells us that a restaurant has "the best food in town." Another sign urges us to listen to the city's "hottest radio station." At home, we find a bright orange sign on the doorknob. It is a printed announcement of the opening of a new pizza restaurant. We turn on the television and see a group of wind-blown surfers gulping a new kind of soft drink.

Advertising is paid for by people who want to inform or influence us. Advertising can educate us about important things. We can learn about health and safety from advertisements. Some advertisements tell us how to avoid diseases like AIDS and that drinking and driving is dangerous. Other advertising tries to affect how we vote. Most advertising tries to sell us things.

Everywhere we go—even at home—we see and hear advertising that influences our decisions about what we wear, eat, and buy. Advertising also affects our choice of transportation, music, and TV programs. We are *consumers* or *customers*—people who buy and use products and services.

Although advertising attracts and influences consumers, we can learn to use advertising to our advantage. Advertising tells us what we can find to buy and at what cost. Advertising gives us facts about products or services and lets us make comparisons. In the following chapters, you will learn about different kinds of advertising, how advertising affects us, and how we can use advertising to make better choices. When you finish reading this book, you will understand how to make advertising work for you.

WHAT IS ADVERTISING?

The purpose of advertising is to persuade people to buy products (such as jeans) or services (such as bus transportation), or to believe a certain point of view. Some kinds of advertising make us think a certain way about a person (the nation's President), a product (shampoo), or an issue (air pollution).

The word *advertising* can be used in several ways. When a person or company tries to persuade people to buy or use a product or service, the person or company is *advertising*. The description of the product or service is called an *advertisement* or *ad*. A group of advertisements can be called *advertising*.

The word *advertising* also is used to describe an individual or group of persons who creates or sells

---

Consumers of all ages are exposed to advertising.

advertisements—or advertising. For example, a person who sells advertising is an *advertising agent.* An *advertising director* is in charge of the people who create advertisements. The advertising agent and advertising director both work for an *advertising agency.* If you asked them what kind of work they do, they might both answer, "I'm in advertising." Actually, they work in the *advertising industry.* This is the part of the business world that creates and sells advertising.

The Beginning of Advertising

People who advertise are called *advertisers.* Through advertising, they seek to sell their product, service, or idea. But the idea of advertising is not new. The first advertisers probably were people who lived in small groups at the beginning of human history. When one person wanted to trade food or an animal skin, he simply told each person in the group. This is called *word-of-mouth advertising.* You could use this kind of advertising if you wanted to trade baseball cards with your friends.

When human groups became larger and people began living in villages, advertisers stood in the center of the village and shouted out their wares. In ancient Egypt, people wrote ads on a plant material called *papyrus* and posted them on walls. Today advertising notices are posted on buildings, buses, and the bulletin boards in supermarkets, Laundromats and the workplace.

Throughout history, people have advertised their businesses with signs showing what product or service they sold. The drawing of a boot hung above the entrance to the shoemaker's shop. The painting of a fish showed people where they could buy seafood. In today's mall, the beauty shop advertises its prices next to a photo of a woman with beautiful hair. A sketch of a fancy five-layer cake attracts today's bride to a specialty bakery.

If you had lived in Europe during the Middle Ages, you might have watched tradespeople perform public plays and *commercials* (spoken advertisements). During the commercial break 600 years ago, you could not have switched channels or zapped through a program taped with your VCR. Instead, you might have heard the tailor stop in the middle of the play to point out that the actors' clothing needed repairs.

The Printing Press

You already know that advertisers have used signs and the spoken word to get their message to customers for centuries. The invention of the printing press around 1450 A.D. helped advertisers reach more people. A printed advertisement such as a *pamphlet* (small booklet) could be handed out to many people. A poster could be printed and put up in many places. Instead of writing and drawing each separately, advertisers had more time to be original. Soon, many ads did more than simply tell

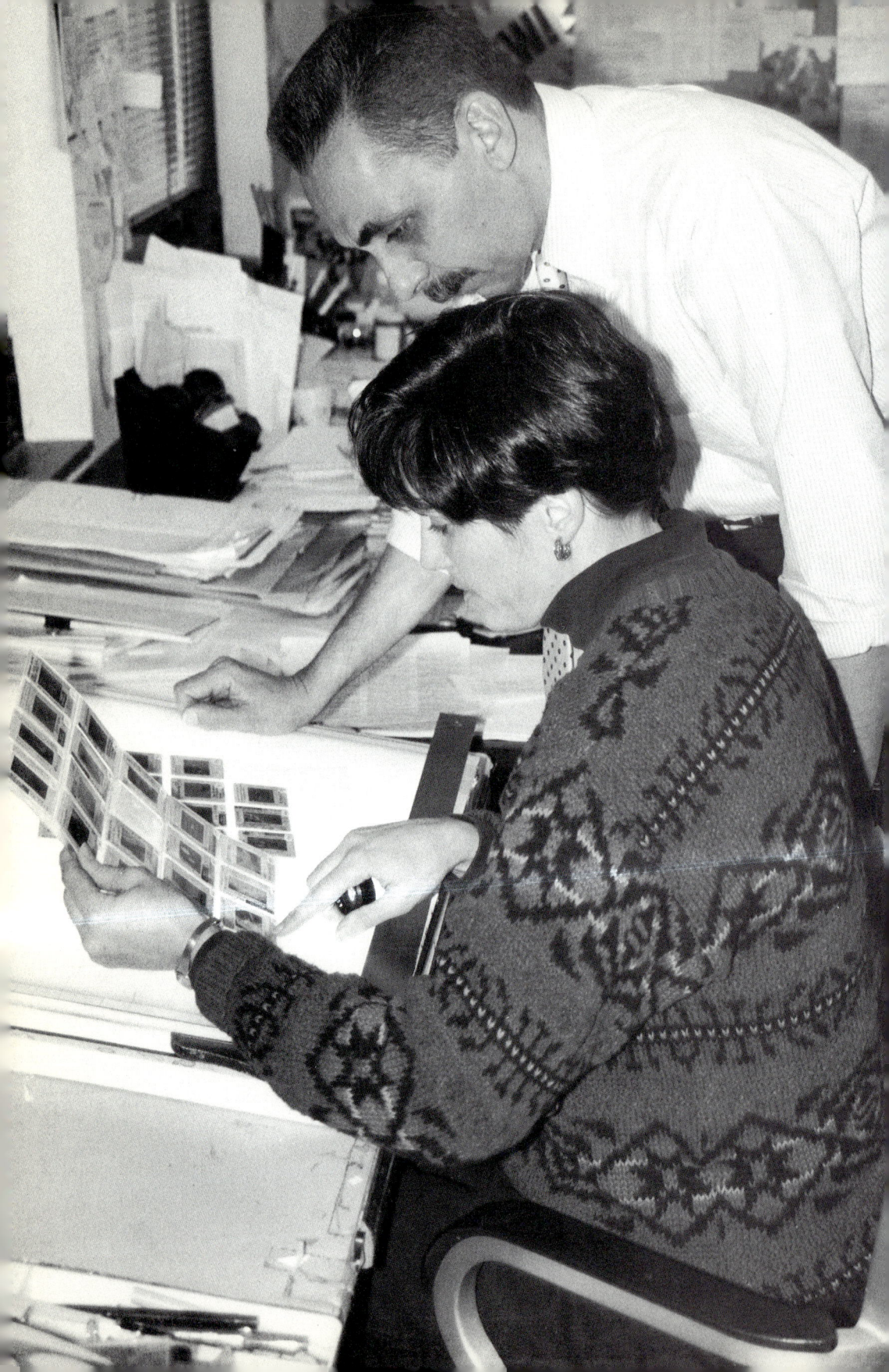

about a product or service. Advertisers began using suggestion and persuasion to influence consumers. Modern advertising had begun!

The people who settled in America brought with them the idea of advertising. In our nation's early years, consumers believed whatever advertisers told them about their products, even though some advertisers were not honest. We may think it funny that people bought "medicated underwear" because an advertisement claimed that wearing the underwear would prevent many diseases. Although ads are more truthful today, we must think carefully about how they affect our decisions about what to buy.

False Advertising

Advertising has grown rapidly over the past century. "It pays to advertise" became the slogan for many businesses. Agencies were formed to sell and create ads. At the same time, consumers began to question the claims made by advertisers. Laws were passed to prevent *false advertising*, or untruthful advertising. False advertising claims that a product or service will do something it really cannot do. Organizations such as the Better Business Bureau (BBB) were formed in many communities to help consumers avoid purchasing items that were falsely advertised. The BBB keeps records of consumers' complaints about businesses. A consumer can check

Advertising agencies create advertisements that have memorable images and phrases.

with the local BBB to find out if a certain business has had complaints against it.

Let's look at how a BBB helped Joanne Harris when she was shopping for a boombox. Joanne saw a local store's advertisement in the newspaper. The ad offered a 10 percent discount on a boombox with a "trade-in" of an old cassette player. Joanne took two cassette players to the store and expected a 20 percent discount—10 percent for each trade-in. But the store manager was willing to give her only 10 percent.

Joanne did not buy the boombox. She went to the BBB office in her town. She showed the store's ad to Kevin Miller, a BBB employee, and explained what had happened at the store. Miller looked in the files and found that other people had made the same complaint when the store advertised a trade-in sale on electric coffeemakers at Christmas time.

Joanne returned to the store and told the manager that the BBB had complaints from several consumers who believed the store's ads promised a 10 percent discount for *each* item traded in. The store manager was surprised to learn that people did not understand the ads. He agreed to give Joanne a 20 percent discount for her two cassette players, but he decided to make future advertisements less confusing. The next time a trade-in discount was advertised, the store ad plainly stated "limit of one trade-in for each purchase."

It was not until the late 1950s that the nation's teenagers became prime targets of the advertising industry. Before that time, advertisements were aimed only at adults. Then research showed that teens were making their own choices about which records, cosmetics, costume jewelry, and magazines to buy. Over the next two decades, more and more families allowed teenagers to buy their own clothing and other higher-priced items. Advertisers began creating many ads aimed at teen consumers.

Advertising research also showed that African-Americans and women were separate consumer groups. Advertisers created ads aimed specifically at these groups. In the 1950s and 1960s, magazines such as *Jet* and *Ebony* sold products manufactured just for African-Americans. Ads in magazines and on TV were aimed at women who held jobs away from home. In the 1970s, for example, ads for frozen dinners and fast-food restaurants replaced those for pots and pans. Because many of today's Americans are concerned about staying healthy and keeping trim, we now see ads for low-calorie snacks and running shoes.

Advertisements show life as it is and as we want it to be. In today's ads, people drive cars that are supposed to be safe as well as fast and good-looking. Some ads suggest that you will be popular if you use a certain shampoo or wear a certain brand of jeans. You see advertisements for many more products and services than your parents or grandparents could buy at your age. Let's see how these products and services are advertised.

TYPES OF ADVERTISING

The advertising industry has several parts. The two most important parts are the consumer and the advertiser. Anyone who buys the products or services that are advertised or accepts an idea that is promoted is a consumer. The advertiser is the one whose products or services are being sold or whose idea is being promoted. The advertiser's brand (product) name, company name, or personal name appears in the ad.

Another part of the advertising industry is the advertising agency or agent. Agents work for agencies and arrange ads for the advertiser.

The final part of advertising is the *media,* which bring advertisements to consumers. The media most used by advertisers are television, radio, newspapers, magazines, and direct mail.

Advertising a special-interest item in a store's flyer may encourage you to shop in a particular store.

The three major types of advertising are *institutional advertisements, product advertisements,* and *public service announcements.*

Institutional Advertising

One purpose of institutional advertising is to improve the image of a business or company. For example, some people believe that processing crude oil into gasoline is harmful to the environment. A gasoline company's institutional advertising might tell the public about the money the company donates each year to help improve the environment. The company hopes to make people think it cares about the environment.

Another purpose of institutional advertising is to keep a company name before the public. For example, a national computer company may sponsor live symphony performances in several cities or on TV. The company's advertising manager may believe that people who enjoy such music are the kinds of people who buy computers. The manager hopes that these consumers will remember the company's name when and if they buy a computer.

Product Advertising

There are four kinds of product advertising. The one we see most often is *consumer advertising.* The other kinds are *professional advertising, trade advertising,* and *industrial advertising.* Each form of product advertising tells about a certain brand, or kind, of product.

Let's see how Joanne Harris used consumer advertising to her advantage.

Joanne wanted to buy the same kind of jeans her best friend got for Christmas. Because Joanne could not afford to pay full price for the jeans, she waited for them to go on sale. Finally, she saw an ad in the newspaper stating that the Denim Shop would sell those $29 jeans for $25.95 for the next week. Another store, Jeanstown, had an ad that said all jeans in the store were reduced by 25 percent for the entire week. Joanne also heard a radio commercial about a discount store that had "the lowest clothing prices in town."

Joanne did not want to go to each store to compare prices. She took a closer look at the newspaper ads. The Jeanstown ad listed the regular price of the jeans as $30. Joanne needed to figure 25 percent of $30 to know what the jeans would sell for on sale. She multiplied $30 by .25 (which is 25 percent), which equals $7.50. This is the result of her investigation:

The Denim Shop
Regular price $29.00   Sale price $25.95

Jeanstown
Regular price $30.00
(minus 25%)   - 7.50
                      $22.50 Sale price $22.50

Now Joanne needed to know the price of the same jeans at the discount store. She learned that their price was $26. She compared her prices again.

The Denim Shop
Regular price $29.00   Sale price $25.95

Jeanstown
Regular Price $30.00   Sale price $22.50

Discount Store
Regular price $26.00   No sale price

Joanne bought her jeans on sale at Jeanstown for the lowest price ($22.50). If she had not waited for the advertised sale, she would have paid more.

Professional advertising is another form of product advertising. It is aimed at people who do specific jobs, like Patti Jones, who is a beautician. Patti reads magazines like *Beauty Education*. The magazines have ads for nail and hair care products that beauticians use on their customers.

Trade advertising also is a form of product advertising. Trade ads are aimed at the people who buy directly from manufacturers (people who make products). Patti's brother, Brian, works at an auto supply store. He sees trade ads for tires in magazines like *Modern Tire Dealer.* Other magazines the store receives advertise auto supplies like brake fluid and car batteries.

—

Comparative shopping can save you money.

Product advertising aimed at manufacturers is called *industrial advertising*. It is printed in business magazines. Sharon Jones, Patti's and Brian's mother, works in the communications department of Northern Steel Company. Mrs. Jones writes ads that appear in magazines read by many automobile manufacturers. The ads are designed to persuade automakers to buy the steel they use from Northern Steel Company.

Public Service Announcements

Another kind of advertisement is the *public service announcement* (PSA). Radio and television stations provide PSAs as free advertising time for nonprofit organizations such as youth clubs, churches, and the U.S. military. If you belong to the YMCA/YWCA or you were a Boy Scout, Girl Scout, or Camp Fire member, you might have joined because you heard a PSA about the group's activities. The U.S. Army, Navy, Air Force, and Marines use PSAs to persuade young people to join the military. By using PSAs, nonprofit organizations can announce information to the public without spending money. The money they save is used for programs.

Newspapers often print *news releases* for nonprofit organizations instead of requiring the groups to buy advertising space. News releases are short news announcements about scheduled events, such as a YMCA basketball tournament, a local high school musical, or a church bazaar.

ADVERTISING MEDIA

The purpose of advertising is to make us want something we may not need (a new car) or to make us choose a certain brand of product. To do this, advertising influences us through our senses. These include seeing, hearing, smelling, tasting, and feeling. When an advertisement affects more than one of our senses, it is *multisensory*. A multisensory ad can influence us more strongly than one that appeals only to one of our senses.

Among the many kinds of advertising media, some are multisensory; others are not. In this chapter we shall learn more about kinds of media and how each one affects consumers.

Television Advertising

Television (TV) commercials reach nearly everyone. Because TV commercials are multisensory, they can influence us almost as much as a person who talks with us face-to-face. TV commercials appeal to our eyes and ears. They use color and motion combined with music and carefully chosen words. They get our attention and affect the way we feel.

We may see the same commercial several times during one program. The commercial may be a *testimonial,* in which a famous person urges us to buy a certain product. When a rock star dances across our TV screen three times in one hour and tells us to buy the kind of jeans he or she is wearing, our emotions are affected. The commercial makes us *feel* a need for the product. We must realize, however, that our admiration of the star doesn't mean we will like the product.

Public television programs have no commercial breaks. Public television is supported by donations from people (the public), by sponsors who use institutional advertising, and by the government. A program's sponsors are mentioned only at the beginning or end. The program has no clever songs or catchy phrases, no reenactment of someone using a product or service. This kind of advertising has less impact because it does not appeal so much to the senses. But we might feel good about the sponsor who pays for a program we enjoy.

—

Our opinions and choices are influenced by advertising.

Radio Advertising

Radio commercials can reach us nearly anywhere—
in the car, at home, while we are walking, or in the
grocery store. Radio advertising influences us because it sounds like a personal message, especially if
we are alone with the voice coming from the radio.
Even when we are only half listening, the repeated
"personal message" gives us the feeling that we
should buy the advertised product or service very
soon. We must realize that everyone listening to
the radio is hearing the same "personal message."
We should ask ourselves if we really want or need
the advertised product or service.

Advertising on public radio stations is like advertising on public television. A program's sponsors
are mentioned only at the beginning or end of the
program. Carol Harris, Joanne's mother, listens to
symphony concerts on public radio every Sunday.
For weeks, she has heard the institutional advertising of the XYZ computer company that sponsors
the broadcast. Because Mrs. Harris enjoys the program, she also feels good about the company.

When the Harris family decides to buy a computer, chances are that Mrs. Harris will look at an
XYZ computer at the store and will probably want
to buy it. She should stop and think about why an
XYZ computer is the one she wants to have. She
should realize that her enjoyment of the musical
program has nothing to do with the quality or price
of computers. She should compare many kinds of
computers before deciding which one to buy.

Magazine Advertising

We have learned that TV commercials and radio commercials are aimed at a certain audience. Some magazine advertising is aimed at a certain group of readers, while other ads have a more general appeal. For example, many different kinds of people read magazines such as *TV Guide* and *People*. The ads are designed to interest a variety of readers. Many magazines, however, are read by people with special interests. Therefore, the ads in these magazines, such as *Motor Trend* and *Postcard Collector*, are aimed at readers with those particular interests.

Like TV ads, some magazine ads appeal to more than one of our senses. While TV ads appeal to our eyes and ears, "scratch-and-sniff" ads appeal to our eyes and nose. Perfume ads that appear in magazines such as *Working Woman* and *Redbook* tell the reader the perfume will make her smell and feel wonderful. But the scratch-and-sniff part of the ad influences the reader the most. The page has a scented area the reader can scratch, smell, and rub onto her wrists. The consumer can sample the perfume's fragrance before buying it.

Newspaper Advertising

Many newspaper readers get information from the ads as well as from the news articles. About 60 percent of the space in newspapers is filled with advertising. Let's see how the Jones family uses newspaper advertising.

Brian Jones is looking for a car. He is comparing the descriptions and the prices of cars in the *classified ads*. Classified ads are the compact advertisements on the last pages of newspapers and some magazines arranged according to subject, such as "Automobiles, Used," "Apartments for Rent," and "Help Wanted."

Brian's mother turns to the newspaper's business pages because she is interested in learning more about insurance. In addition to the articles, Mrs. Jones reads the *display ads*. These are medium-sized or large ads that usually include a photo or drawing. Mrs. Jones reads the insurance ads to learn the names of agents who sell the kind of insurance she wants to buy.

Once a week, the newspaper has a special section of grocery store advertisements. The Jones family compares the prices in the ads to learn which stores have the lowest prices. They cut out coupons that will reduce the price of some of the products.

Direct Mail Advertising

Many families receive advertisements in the mail. Some people call this "junk mail." The correct name is *direct mail advertising*. It includes postcards, letters, catalogs, newsletters, and brochures. Let's look at the direct mail advertising the Jones family received one day.

—

Sometimes we are overloaded with unwanted advertising.

At work, Mrs. Jones received a catalog from a computer company and a brochure from a local office supply store that was having a sale. In the mailbox at home, Mrs. Jones found a letter from a magazine publisher. The letter invited her to enter a sweepstakes, and to subscribe to several magazines.

Brian's mail included a bright green postcard that invited him to a stock car rally. Patti received a newsletter from a political group, asking her to become a member.

All direct mail advertising is designed to influence the people who read it. The computer company tried to make readers want the newest computer equipment by showing photos and giving descriptions in a catalog. The office supply store hoped their sale would attract customers. The sweepstakes was a way of selling magazines. The publishing company knew that some people would order magazines when they entered the sweep-stakes. The group that was holding the stock car rally knew that Brian might join the group if he was invited to their activities. Patti's newsletter had articles that looked like news, but they were written in a way meant to affect people's thinking on certain political issues. The organization hoped readers would be influenced to vote a certain way and to pay for membership in the group. The membership fees would be used for printing more newsletters and influencing more people.

Store-front ads try to catch your eye and spark your interest.

Outdoor Advertising

When our car is traveling along a highway or we are waiting for a bus, we see large outdoor signs called *billboards* advertising everything from soft drinks to cigarettes. You already know this kind of advertising goes back to the days of the ancient Egyptians. It was in the late 1800s, however, that companies began putting advertising on large wooden boards. The ads were called "bills," so the boards became known as "billboards." Artists painted the advertisements on the billboards back then, and some still do, but most of the billboards around today are greatly enlarged photographs.

Today's outdoor advertising also includes electric signs and posters in store windows and on the sides of buildings. Every few years, some buildings are covered with *political posters* urging us to cast our vote for a certain candidate. When we see the same outdoor advertising message many times, we remember it.

Outdoor advertising also includes the signs on the inside and outside of buses and on the bumper stickers we put on cars. Another form of outdoor advertising is the electrical message that promotes a product or service along with giving the time and temperature. We see this kind of advertising on bank buildings and at the entrance to a mall. The bank advertisement may tell us to put our money into a savings account. The mall advertising tells us when a special event, such as an antique show, takes place or which stores are having sales.

Other Kinds of Advertising

There are many kinds of *novelty advertising:*
bumper stickers, coffee mugs, calendars, pens, pencils, caps, match books, "raisin people," and key
chains. Many novelty advertising items are given to
customers, but consumers buy some novelty items,
such as T-shirts and jackets.

Business cards are a way of reminding consumers
about a product or service. These small cards give
the name and business phone number of a person
who sells a product or service. (The person's home
phone number may also be listed.) A person who
gives out business cards hopes that the customer
will carry the card in a handy place. Some people
keep other people's business cards in a file on their
desk or in an appointment book.

Coupons and *premiums* also are forms of advertising. A coupon encourages a consumer to buy a
certain brand of a product by offering to reduce the
price by a certain amount. A premium is something
the customer gets along with the purchase.

Premiums include *rebates* and *prizes.* A rebate is
the return of part of the purchase price to the consumer. For example, one side of a cereal box might
have a form offering 25 cents back for every proof
of purchase you send to the company with the
form. The proof of purchase usually is the universal
bar code the cashier scans at the checkout counter.
A prize premium is something extra the consumer
gets with the product, such as a pack of baseball
cards in a box of cereal.

Wake up to freshness.

HOW TO HEAR
THE PITCH

Advertising sells products, services, and ideas by affecting the way we feel—usually the way we feel about ourselves. It often makes us want something we don't need, such as a new car or lunch at the local fast-food restaurant.

If we analyze, or examine, an advertisement, we can find out how it affects us. To analyze an ad, we need to understand advertising techniques, or methods used to influence our feelings. These techniques include *transfer, misleading generalities, association*, and *conformity*.

The technique called *transfer* makes us think of a certain image when we think of a certain product. For example, Marlboro cigarettes were advertised for many years by the Marlboro man, who was

---

Manufacturers take every opportunity to make the public aware of their products.

rugged and masculine. Some men smoked Marlboro cigarettes because they wanted to be rugged, too. The smokers transferred the image of the Marlboro man's masculinity to the cigarettes he advertised. When we analyze cigarette ads, we realize that strength and ruggedness do not depend on smoking cigarettes. In fact, the small print in cigarette ads and on packs warns that smoking causes certain health problems—like the one that killed the Marlboro man.

Misleading generalities make us think something that is not true by telling us something that is true. For example, if an ad tells us that no other cereal has more vitamins than Crunchy-Munch, we might think that Crunchy-Munch is higher in vitamins than other cereals. But when we analyze the information in the ad, we realize that other cereals could have the same amount of vitamins as Crunchy-Munch. To learn the complete truth, we must compare the list of vitamins on a box of Crunchy-Munch with the lists on other cereal brands.

Some advertisements barely mention the product they are selling. Through *association*, these ads create a mood that is supposed to make us want the product. One carpet company's advertisement shows two well-dressed people enjoying an elaborate dinner in a beautiful house. The woman and man are enjoying themselves so much that they do something outrageous—they have a food fight. The carpet brand is mentioned only at the end of the ad. When we analyze this, we realize that a mood of elegant, outrageous fun has nothing to do with the kind of carpeting we might buy.

The voice in a commercial for an amusement park says, "Follow the crowd to Valley Fair." A Pepsi advertisement tells us, "You got the right one, baby." These ads use the *conformity* technique. It is based on the idea that we want to be part of a group. The advertisers believe we will buy their product or service because it's the popular thing to do. To analyze this kind of advertising, we should ask ourselves several questions. "What is right for me?" "Would I be interested in the product even if no one else was?"

Advertising can influence us by affecting several different kinds of feelings. When we see an advertisement that shows a family eating hot soup on a snowy day, we feel warm and cozy. An ad that shows two people enjoying a cup of tea together brings out feelings of friendship, trust, and security. Such ads make us want to buy the advertised brands of soup and tea so that we will feel the same way.

Tobacco and liquor advertising appeals to our desire for pleasure and excitement. When Joanne Harris saw an ad that said one brand of cigarettes was "alive with pleasure," she got the message that the brand gave smokers more pleasure than other cigarettes. Then Joanne realized there was a deeper meaning. By using the word "alive," the advertiser was influencing people to ignore the fact that smoking causes diseases that often end in death. Ads for beer and wine also use the idea of pleasure to sell the products. They also influence people to ignore the fact that alcohol is a factor in many automobile accidents and that drinking liquor can result in certain diseases.

Advertising also plays on feelings we do not like, such as fear, shame, or embarrassment. Advertisers use these feelings to influence us to buy products such as deodorants, mouthwash, and shampoo. Let's see how Joanne Harris analyzed a TV commercial involving a teenager.

In one scene, Joanne saw a girl who was sad because she was sitting alone at a high school basketball game. Later, the girl's older sister suggested the girl should "do something" with her hair. After the girl used Super Fantastic shampoo and conditioner, she was surrounded by boys at the next game. Joanne realized that the commercial had more than one message. The first message was, "Super Fantastic hair care products are good to buy and to use." The next message was, "Super Fantastic products will make you popular." Then Joanne realized there was a third message that was harder to see. It was, "If you don't use Super Fantastic products, you will be alone." The advertiser wanted to make teenage girls feel afraid (and embarrassed) to be alone. After thinking about the ad, Joanne realized that advertising messages can be foolish. Buying a certain brand of shampoo would not affect her popularity!

When you unwrap a new purchase, you may find advertising for special offers on related products.

Advertisements also can appeal to our feelings of ambition, competition, vanity, envy, or greed. These kinds of ads use words like, "You're worth it" to sell haircoloring, and "You've come a long way, baby" to sell cigarettes. The U.S. Army advertises for new recruits with the message "Be all you can be," and the U.S. Marine Corps is looking for "a few good men." The message in these ads is that if we do what the ad suggests, it will make us better than other people.

Some advertisements seem to appeal to our logic instead of our feelings. These ads may use *the permissible lie.* The permissible lie lets us decide what to think based on what we see and hear in an ad. For example, when an advertiser tells us that Tummy-Soother medicine gives fast relief from an upset stomach, we must decide how fast "fast" really is. Another example of the permissible lie is an ad that tells us Tiptop potato chips are "the perfect answer to the munchies."

Some lies, however, are not permissible. For example, a car manufacturer advertises a compact car with "plenty of leg room." In the ad, a tall basketball player sits comfortably in the car. To be honest, the ad must show a regular model of the car. If the advertiser uses a car that was made to look the same but has more leg room because it has no engine, that is *deceptive advertising.* If the deceptive advertising is discovered, the Federal Trade Commission, which is a government agency, will make the car advertiser change the ad.

Another illegal kind of advertising is called *bait and switch*. An item is advertised at an unusually low price. When you try to buy it, the sales clerk says the item is sold out. Or the clerk tells you the item is of such poor quality that it is not worth even the low price. The clerk tries to get you to buy a higher-priced item. If you want the sale item, you should insist on buying it. If the store is out of the sale item, ask for a *raincheck*. This is a piece of paper signed by the clerk or store manager that says you may buy the item at the sale price after the sale is over. If you have a problem with bait and switch advertising, report it to the Better Business Bureau or another consumer protection organization.

When we vote, we are influenced by *political advertising*. Political advertising sells us an idea or an image by telling us what we want to hear. In 1992, when Bill Clinton wanted to be elected President of the United States, he used political advertising to his advantage. He told voters he knew they wanted change and that he was the person who could make that change happen. His advertised image was that he understood ordinary people and that he would be the kind of president they wanted. He was elected.

When we see or hear advertising—for a cereal or for a President—we can look for facts in the ad. We can analyze the ad to see how it influences our feelings. We can ask ourselves questions about the advertising. By doing this, we can use advertising instead of letting it use us.

CONCLUSION: WHAT YOU HAVE LEARNED

Let's take a look at what you have learned about advertising. You know that advertising informs and influences us about ideas, products, and services. You understand that its purpose is to get people to buy products or services or to believe a certain point of view. You have learned how advertising began and the many ways in which it grew.

You know the difference between institutional advertising, product advertising, and public service announcements. You also have learned that product advertising includes consumer, professional, trade, and industrial advertising.

Advertising can direct our attention, but it is up to the individual to make informed decisions.

You are aware of the differences between advertising on TV and radio stations, in magazines, and newspapers, by direct mail, on billboards, and by other means.

Advertising ideas are researched, tested, and approved. There is a lot of money spent on advertising and a lot of money to be earned from advertising. It is a huge industry that affects our daily lives.

One of the most important things to know about advertising is that it *intends* to affect your feelings. It wants a reaction from you, the consumer; it wants you to buy or use whatever is being advertised.

As long as you keep in mind the techniques being used to influence you, you can make informed decisions. If you continue to ask questions and compare information, you can use advertising to your own advantage.

GLOSSARY
EXPLAINING NEW WORDS

advertisement Public announcement designed to sell or promote a product, service, or idea; also called an ad.

advertising 1) The act of creating or selling through advertisements; 2) a group of advertisements.

advertising agency Business that creates and sells advertisements.

advertising agent Person who sells advertising.

advertising director The person in charge of people who create advertisements.

advertising industry The part of the business world that describes and promotes products, services, and ideas through advertisements.

audience The people who watch or listen to a program.

bait and switch Advertising that promotes a product or service at a low cost, with the idea that the consumer will buy a higher-priced product or service instead.

billboard Board, usually outdoors, on which advertisements are put.

business card Small card giving information about a person who sells a product or service.

classified advertisement Small advertisement on the last pages of newspapers and some magazines.

commercial Spoken advertisement.

consumer Person who buys and uses products and services.

consumer advertising Advertising aimed at consumers.

coupon Piece of paper that provides the consumer with a lower price on a product or service.

customer Consumer, usually a person who buys goods or services at a certain store.

deceptive advertising Use of unreal situations to make consumers believe a product can do something it cannot do; similar to false advertising.

direct mail advertising Advertisements that are mailed to homes or businesses.

display advertisement Printed advertisement that usually includes drawings or photos.

false advertising Untruthful advertising.

industrial advertising Advertising aimed at manufacturers.

institutional advertising Advertising designed to improve the image of a business or industry.

manufacturer's coupon Coupon distributed by the company that makes a product.

media Various means of communications.

misleading advertising Advertising that uses something that is true to make us believe something that is not true.

multisensory Affecting more than one of our five senses.

news release Printed news announcement about the activities of a group or organization.

novelty advertising Advertising on items such as T-shirts, key chains, and coffee mugs.

pamphlet Small booklet.

permissible lie Advertisement that lets us decide what to think based on what we see and hear in the ad.

political advertising (1) advertising by people running for election to a political office; (2) advertising about political issues.

premium Something the customer gets free along with the product he or she buys.

product advertising Advertising that promotes a certain product or brand of product.

professional advertising Advertising aimed at people who do certain jobs or have certain professions.

program sponsor Television or radio advertisers.

public radio Radio stations that are supported by donations from the public.

public service announcement (PSA) (1) Announcement made on radio or television, usually by a nonprofit organization; (2) free advertisement.

public television Television stations that are supported by donations from the public.

raincheck A piece of paper that permits you to buy an item at the sale price after the sale is over.

rebate The return of part of the purchase price to the customer.

store coupon Coupon distributed by a store that sells a product.

testimonial Statement, usually made by a well-known person, that promotes a product, service, or idea.

trade advertising Advertising aimed at the people who buy directly from manufacturers.

viewer profile Information about the age, sex, income, and buying interests of people who watch television.

FOR FURTHER READING

Frisch, Carlienne. *Advertising*. Vero Beach, FL: Rourke Enterprises, Inc., 1989.

Klein, David. *How Do You Know It's True?* New York: Scribner's, 1984.

Schmitt, Lois. *Smart Spending*. New York: Macmillan, 1989.

The Role of Advertising in America. New York: Association of National Advertisers, Inc., 1992.

Wake, Susan. *Advertising*. Ada, OK: Garrett Educational Corp., 1990.

Weiss, Anne E. *The School on Madison Avenue*. New York: E.P. Dutton, 1980.

INDEX

About the Author

Carlienne Frisch has written books on such diverse topics as pet care, European countries, and the author Maud Hart Lovelace. Before becoming a free-lance writer, she worked as an editor for a farm magazine and in public relations for nonprofit organizations.

The author is president of the Friends of the Minnesota Valley Regional Library and a member of the Society of Children's Book Writers, Habitat for Humanity, and the local historical society. She enjoys reading mysteries and historical novels. She also collects, decorates, and furnishes dollhouses.

Ms. Frisch and her husband, Robert, have four adult children. They share their home with York, a tortoise-shell cat.

Photo Credits
Page 10: Blackbirch Graphics, Inc.; all other photos on cover and in book by Mary Lauzon.

Design & Production by Blackbirch Graphics, Inc.